LIFESHAPES

Discipleship The Way Jesus Did It

The Circle ───

CHOOSING *to* LEARN *from* LIFE

WORKBOOK

MIKE BREEN

NexGen® is an imprint of
Cook Communications Ministries, Colorado Springs, CO 80918
Cook Communications, Paris, Ontario
Kingsway Communications, Eastbourne, England

First printing 2006
Printed in South Korea
1 2 3 4 5 6 7 8 9 10 Printing/Year 10 09 08 07 06 05

Cover Design: Brand Navigation, LLC

Mike Breen is the creator and developer of the LifeShapes material (formerly called LifeSkills) and the eight (8) shapes
as a memorable method of discipleship.

ISBN: 0-78144-295-8

Around and around we go. Job, workouts, errands, kids, an occasional date, yard work, money stresses, relationships gone wrong—it all adds up. We're living at merry-go-round speed. Just when we stop feeling dizzy and things begin to come into focus, someone shoves the merry-go-round again. A car accident. An illness. A foolish mistake. An uncontrolled temper. A missed appointment. These are the things that keep the merry-go-round spinning.

Many times we can't stop these things from happening. But we can learn from them. That's what this study is all about—making an intentional choice to learn lessons about discipleship from the events that happen when we least expect them. The Learning Circle, the first of eight *LifeShapes,* teaches us how to learn from these moments by giving us a process that makes sure we get all the way around the circle. We'll see how Jesus taught his disciples to learn from their experiences, and we'll see how we can learn the same way.

WHY LIFESHAPES?

LifeShapes takes advantage of our tendency to remember what we see longer than we remember what we hear. Biblical principles connected to basic shapes help you remember how to follow Jesus' example in every aspect of your life. With these eight shapes, you can learn to live as Jesus' disciple:

- **Circle:** Choosing to Learn from Life
- **Semi-Circle:** Living in Rhythm with Life
- **Triangle:** Balancing the Relationships of Life
- **Square:** Defining the Priorities of Life
- **Pentagon:** Knowing Your Role in Life
- **Hexagon:** Praying as a Way of Life
- **Heptagon:** Practicing the Principles of a Vital Life
- **Octagon:** Living a Life with a Mission

These aspects of kingdom life are easy enough to show using simple shapes, yet deep enough that we will never reach the end of learning even one of them. In this workbook, you will study the Learning Circle and explore choosing to learn from the experiences of your life. But remember, this is just one part of the discipleship process. Additional studies on other shapes can take you deeper.

LIFE TOGETHER

LifeShapes is relational. Jesus understood the human need for companionship. His life and ministry here on earth was done

with a group of believers he called his friends. Jesus lived out for us God's ideal for his followers— authentic community.

While individuals can benefit from using this workbook along with the book, *Choosing to Learn from Life,* this study is built to encourage the community aspect of *LifeShapes.* So if you're not connected to a group at the moment, find at least one other person—a friend, co-worker, spouse, or family member—who is willing to do this study along with you. *Choosing to Learn from Life Small Group Resource* contains a Teaching DVD, a PowerPoint® presentation, a Leader's Guide

with additional teaching commentary, as well as a copy of the book, *Choosing to Learn from Life.*

LifeShapes is also designed to be multipliable—the Matthew 28 principle. After Jesus says, "Come!" he tells us to "Go" and teach others what we have learned from walking with him. With LifeShapes, there aren't a lot of principles to memorize or a twelve-step program for spiritual maturity to follow. It's simply a visual set of reminders of the things Jesus wants us to learn. As you begin to learn from these shapes, you'll want to share them with others.

USING THIS WORKBOOK

The eight sessions in this workbook are designed to take you deeper in your relationship with God. You will learn a new vocabulary to help you understand and describe the biblical principles of discipleship. Each session is divided up into three sections: Reflect, Respond, and React.

Reflect

This section encourages you to think about real-life situations related to the Circle. Sharing personal experiences will help you feel connected with others in your group. Reflect also helps you to focus on what God wants you to learn so you are not just listening to what someone else is learning. Reflect asks questions to help you personalize the message.

Respond

New material is presented here, and you are given opportunity to answer questions about the material. You will also discuss important points with a learning technique called Huddles. It takes at least two to Huddle, but a Huddle may have several people in it. Huddles are a time for teaching and community-building. We learn best and benefit most when we engage with others in the learning process. Be honest and vulnerable—so that your learning experience will stick.

React

This is where it gets personal. We know you are going to be challenged to change during this study. That's what happens when we are confronted with God's Word. In React, you will be asked to take what you've learned and apply it to your own life. As you contemplate the personal challenge, take time to share it with someone in the group who can encourage you in your walk of faith. We want you to go away from each session with a plan for extending the lesson into your everyday life.

A PASSIONATE LIFE

You can experience more from your Christian life. *LifeShapes* is simple, but it's not easy. You're passionate about something that you care about deeply, something that stirs deep emotions in you, something that you feel right to your core. Jesus is inviting you to join him—he will guide you, he will walk beside you, he will teach you all you want to know, but he won't settle for less than all of you. Join him in the passionate pursuit of discipleship.

A passionate walk with Jesus.

A passionate faith that spills over into everything you do.

A passionate energy for the kingdom of God.

A passionate conviction to minister to the needs around you.

A passionate search for others ready to meet Jesus.

A PASSIONATE LIFE.

1 "LEARN FROM ME"

IN THIS SESSION, YOU WILL:

Learn that Jesus really is the answer to life's challenges

•

Explore the different ways we try to live a fulfilling life

•

Discover the refreshment that comes from living in God's kingdom

•

Form a plan to carry the right tools for a meaningful spiritual life

You know you want a more meaningful life, filled with a sense of purpose and direction, where you know you are doing exactly what God made you to do. You're just not sure how to go about getting it. The good news is you don't have to accomplish this on your own! Jesus invites you to learn from him how to find meaning in your experiences and grow each day to be more like him.

SCRIPTURAL BASIS:

- **Matthew 11:28–30** — *"Come to me, all you who are weary and burdened, and I will give you rest. Take my yoke upon you and learn from me, for I am gentle and humble in heart, and you will find rest for your souls. For my yoke is easy and my burden is light."*

THINKING AHEAD:

- What kind of burdens does Jesus want us to give him?

_____

_____

_____

- What do we get in exchange when we bring our burdens to Jesus?

_____

_____

_____

IN GOOD COMPANY

THE FILM *In Good Company* (starring Topher Grace) tells the story of Carter Duryea. Duryea is a 26 year-old whiz kid of a multinational conglomerate, GLOBECOM. He is promoted to the head of the ad sales department of *Sports America Magazine*, GLOBECOM's latest acquisition. To complicate the plot, this business success coincides with the disintegration of his marriage. Duryea is being groomed for greatness at GLOBECOM. He's under pressure to produce big things. In reality he is lonely, insecure, and unprepared for life. His ideas and decisions cause conflict with the *Sports America* team.

At the close of the film Duryea loses his position and decides to start over. But before he leaves, he makes a profound admission to his colleague, Dan Foreman (played by Dennis Quaid). He thanks Foreman and says that no one had ever cared enough to give him a hard time before or to teach him the things that he really needed to know about life.[1]

In fact, the entire film is about change. It serves as an extraordinary example of how mankind is so often unwilling to accept or implement change in life. Then, when faced with the consequences of those decisions, such as a crumbling marriage or unclear career path, we are forced to make clear-cut decisions, change or don't change. Carter Duryea spends most of his time promising change but resisting true transformation. He deals with all kinds of significant moments in which he is presented with an opportunity to change. In the end, he finally learns that his own personal happiness and fruitfulness as a human being depends on his ability to learn and grow from the challenges he faces.

—from ***Choosing to Learn from Life***, Chapter 1

---

1 Paul Weitz, *In Good Company*, DVD, directed by Paul Weitz (Hollywood, CA: Universal, 2004).

Take a few minutes to answer the following questions:

➲ When is a time your life felt out of control?

_____

_____

_____

➲ How well-equipped do you feel for dealing with the challenges of your life as it is today? Explain.

_____

_____

_____

➲ Is there a person in your life who isn't afraid to challenge you in areas of your life that may be questionable? Describe your relationship with this person.

_____

_____

_____

ALL WE HAVE TO DO is pick up a couple of books or watch television to get a picture of our culture's quest to be better and better. "Reality shows" point out the desperate search for meaning and happiness. People go on these shows to be better dressers, better spouses, better parents, or richer people.

We soon see that we are not isolated in our desire to live our lives to the fullest. Some of us, though, don't try to get fixed. Instead we want to escape. We watch sports on TV, remembering our high school or college days. Or we engage in the world of computer games. It's a world away from a life that we can do nothing about and where circumstances never seem to change.

 During the teaching time, Huddles extend the learning experience by encouraging interaction in small groups of 2 or 3.

 ➲ When you run into tough or challenging situations, do you intentionally look for quick ways to "get fixed" or to completely escape? Why do you think this is?

_____

_____

We Christians go to our churches and Bible studies looking for answers. "Jesus is the answer." With our heads, we believe that. Experientially, it's a different story. What does that mean on a day-to-day basis? How is Jesus the answer when you can't keep up with your bills no matter how hard you work? How is Jesus the answer when a difficult child frays at the garment of your family life? Even in good times we often wonder the same thing. Was Jesus really a part of me getting that new job? Is this new car really a blessing from God or just a result of my hard work? The question is not one of knowledge but of application. But we can't admit that, can we? We can't let the people around us—especially other Christians—know that we haven't figured out how to apply the only true answer. So we carry on, wondering, frustrated, indifferent, and living in the shadow of the passionate life that Jesus offers but that we have rarely experienced.

→HUDDLES←

➲ Evaluate how authentic you are with the people around you. Explain.

_____

_____

_____

_____

Being a Christian doesn't necessarily mean you've got life all figured out. And it doesn't mean that you live life perfectly. Trying to do that will just get you tired. Listen to these words from Jesus:

"Come to me, all you who are weary and burdened, and I will give you rest. Take my yoke upon you and learn from me, for I am gentle and humble in heart, and you will find rest for your souls. For my yoke is easy and my burden is light."

—Matthew 11:28–30

The One whom we know to be The Answer offers us an invitation. "Learn from me." When we're tired of the ruts that we are stuck in and the inability to make decisions and work through circumstances of life, we have hope: Learn from Jesus. Is there any better teacher? We spend a lot of time reading books and listening to CDs that claim to have the power to transform our lives. But how do we know which ones will work best for us, or even if the teachings are biblically sound? We tend to forget that, buried beneath all the books and resources of our collection, lies the one and only teacher who can show us everything we need: Jesus.

→HUDDLES←

➲ Write down or discuss your personal interpretation of Matthew 11:28-30.

_____

_____

CHECK YOUR TOOL BELT

THE LEARNING CIRCLE helps us learn in the same way Jesus taught his disciples to understand the world. And since we've got their lives in writing, we can learn to understand Jesus a little better from their experiences. However, when it comes to our own lives, we don't automatically learn just because we have experiences. We learn by studying and reflecting—intentionally choosing to learn. We learn by choosing to enter the Learning Circle.

The Learning Circle is a tool that is meant to be both memorable and repeatable. It's a tool that you can pull out and use in many different situations, just as if you had a hammer and screwdriver hanging from your belt. If you don't wear your tool belt, you start to think you don't need it. You forget about the tools that could be right at your fingertips and try to do

PERSONAL CHALLENGE

➤ In what areas of your life do you personally need to choose to learn from your experiences?

_____

_____

➤ What changes do you think might happen in your life if you made such a choice?

_____

_____

➤ What tools or techniques do you personally have in place right now that help you recognize the need for life-change and then implement those changes?

_____

_____

things the hard way—and probably hurt yourself in the process!

All too often we only go halfway around the Circle, then we forget about the rest of the tools we have available to complete the job. God wants us to be a completed project—not something left unfinished. He will continue to produce events in our lives that seem to us the same lesson over and over again. Only when we make it through the entire Circle do we begin to see life changing results.

Be ready to share in the next session about your experiences of choosing to learn this week.

PERSONAL CHALLENGE

➡ Which part of the Circle is hardest for you to go through? Why?

_____

_____

_____

_____

_____

_____

2 WHEN TIME STANDS STILL

**IN THIS SESSION,
YOU WILL:**

Define and learn to recognize
kairos moments

•

Explore the process of learning
from *kairos* moments

•

Discover how to see
God's kingdom at work
in *kairos* moments

•

Form a plan to welcome
an individual *kairos* moment

Time. Either it crawls slowly when you're waiting for something exciting, or it flies by when you're living life at merry-go-round speed. Nearly every day we wish we had more time for something or other—relaxing, hanging with the kids, reading, exercise, cooking, or chores. But we only get so many minutes in a day. We have to learn to pay attention to the ones that are truly important—the ones that have the potential to change our lives.

SCRIPTURAL BASIS:

- **Mark 1:15** — *"The time has come," [Jesus] said. "The kingdom of God is near. Repent and believe the good news!"*

THINKING AHEAD:

- What four key words do you see in this verse?

_____

_____

_____

_____

- Describe an experience that seemed to change your life in a moment.

_____

_____

_____

_____

KEY WORDS:

Kairos

•

Time

•

Kingdom

•

Repent

•

Believe

OUT OF CONTROL

DO YOU EVER feel as if you're living on a merry-go-round? That life is happening to you, and it's going by so fast you don't know what to focus on? Life is a challenge. Every day we have the same number of minutes and hours of time. Some of those moments may actually be beyond our control, and we have to step back and admit that. But they're never beyond God's control.

As a follower and friend of Jesus, you want your life to count—to have a purpose and meaning. The world offers material gain,

temporary success, and fleeting recognition, but that's just not enough. You desire to leave a legacy where all that you did in this world, whether in your career, your family life, or your ministry, makes a difference in the eternal lives of other people. That is living in the kingdom of God which is a whole different story.

Living in the kingdom is not a fleeting experience. It lasts forever. At the very beginning of his ministry, Jesus tells of a great opportunity: God's kingdom is within our reach. Jesus tells us just what we

have to do: go through a process of repentance and belief. The process can be challenging—even painful. But through this process we learn how to follow Jesus into the kingdom. That's when life starts to make sense.

—from *A Passionate Life*,
Chapter 3

Take a few minutes to answer the following questions:

➔ Reflect on the larger periods of time or seasons in your life. During which stages did you feel the most significance in your life? Why?

_____

_____

_____

_____

➔ What do you think determines whether your life has purpose or meaning?

_____

_____

_____

➔ What is one aspect of your life that outwardly shows that you belong to the kingdom of God?

_____

_____

_____

AS YOU LEARN about *kairos* moments together with your group, fill in key words in the sections that follow.

Jesus broke into actual human history. He is not a theoretical religious figure. He walked the roads of Galilee and Judea at a specific point in time, and time has never been the same since then. Jesus began his ministry with a very short sermon—a sermon that is the summary statement of all his teaching and ideas for the coming few years. This message sets the stage for all he is about to say and do.

> *After John was put in prison, Jesus went into Galilee, proclaiming the good news of God.*
> *"The time has come," he said. "The kingdom of God is near. Repent and believe the good news!"*
> —*Mark 1:14–15*

In these sentences we discover how Jesus helped his disciples understand the world and to learn from their experiences. These two verses fix Jesus in chronological time—after John was put in prison—and summarize his message—the message that is at the heart of the Learning Circle. Let's take the time to dig a little deeper to really understand what Jesus is saying to us.

Mark 1:15 contains four key words for the Learning Circle:

1. _____

2. _____

3. _____

4. _____

In English, we have the word "time" and we use it many different ways. Greek, the original language of the New Testament, has many words for time with specific meanings. The two most common are:

Kairos ~~Time made you stop or challenged you~~

_____ meaning _____ ; and

_____ meaning _____ .

Chronos is the kind of time that is sequential, calendar time, wristwatch time. *Chronos* is the kind of time we would use in the question: "What time is it?" or "What time are we eating dinner tonight?" It's the kind of time where you're conscious of the sequence of ongoing time, how long something takes, measured in minutes or hours.

→HUDDLES← *During the teaching time, Huddles extend the learning experience by encouraging interaction in small groups of 2 or 3.*

→HUDDLES← ➲ Write down your own example of *chronos* time.

_____

Kairos is completely different. *Kairos* is event time, crisis time, the kind of time that we would use in the statement, "That was a great time last night" or "Didn't we have a good time the other day?" "What a time that was!" You are not aware of the clock when it's *kairos* time. In that moment time seems to _____

_____ .

→HUDDLES←   ➲ Think of some of the significant events that have taken place in your life. List several here.

1. _____

2. _____

3. _____

➲ How did these experiences affect your life after that point?

_____

_____

These were *kairos* events. These were occasions when *chronos* time was of no importance. You weren't watching the clock because that wasn't the kind of time that mattered.

Kairos events can either be _____ or _____ experiences. They can be times of celebration and joy or times of pain and sadness. *Kairos* marks a significant _____ in your life.

Think about the day you graduated from college or began a new job. You may not remember how long the ceremony was, but it was definitely an event when time stood still. *Kairos.*

Maybe you remember the day you got engaged or married. *Kairos.*

That promotion at work changed the way your family lives. *Kairos.*

A death in the family changed your role and relationships. *Kairos.*

→**HUDDLES**← ◯ How would you recognize a *kairos* event in the future?

→**HUDDLES**← ◯ Choose a *kairos* moment and tell how you responded to it and whether it was positive or negative.

When we look for them, we realize *kairos* events take place everywhere! We go to a restaurant, and it is a terrific meal or a dismal stress. We're sitting at an intersection, and we look at the wrong set of lights. We think that they're green, we move and then we realize the mistake. We have a near miss on the freeway. We have an argument or a challenge in our lives, and it causes us some kind of crisis. We have great times, and we have awful times.

→**HUDDLES**← ◯ Think of a *kairos* moment that was particularly painful. Share how you were able to grow spiritually through that experience.

EVERYDAY OPPORTUNITIES

SO WE LEARN to recognize *kairos* events. Now what? What do we do with them? We might be tempted to file them away in the back of our minds and ignore them, even forget them, especially if they have a negative effect. We may think through the events that led to the kairos moment so that we never find ourselves in that situation again. But when a *kairos* event has a positive effect, we want to draw it out as long as possible. We relive the moment again and again. We look at pictures or mementos and remember the feelings, the pleasure of the experience.

Kairos presents an opportunity. This takes God out of the boxes of our Sunday school classes, our Bible studies, and services where we may have stored him. God can and wants to impact every part of our lives. With every occasion in your life, whether a positive event or negative, Jesus gives you an opportunity to move forward in discipleship. It's a great opportunity for you to grow as a person; it's a

PERSONAL CHALLENGE

⊙ Write down a *kairos* event you have experienced recently. How did you respond?

_____

_____

_____

_____

⊙ Looking back, how do you wish you had responded to your *kairos* moment?

_____

_____

_____

_____

wonderful opportunity for you to step into the process of learning the way that Jesus teaches. It's an opportunity for God to intervene and for you to learn from Jesus.

The Lord wants each of us to learn how to make the most of each event. When we learn from these experiences, we enter the kingdom of God afresh. We receive anew what it means to grow in him.

Be ready to share in the next session about your *kairos* experiences this week.

⬤ Write down one specific area of your life where you would like the Lord to show you a *kairos* moment this week so you can learn from it.

_____

_____

_____

_____

_____

_____

3 THE RETURN OF THE KING

IN THIS SESSION, YOU WILL:

Learn that the kingdom of God is present now

•

Explore the relationship of *kairos* and *kingdom*

•

Discover the role of repentance and faith in the process of learning

•

Form a plan to examine a personal *kairos*

When you get up in the morning, you think you know what your day will be like. Most days are routine, but other days, the whole world seems to change in a moment. Situations at work, school, or home take an unexpected turn, for better or for worse, and you are left feeling caught off guard. How do you respond when things go wrong—or when things go more right than you expected? Do you use those instances to reflect on your life, or do you simply shrug them off and move on? In all of these circumstances, the kingdom of God is near. God has made his presence known in your life and has a significant lesson for you. Are you ready to learn it?

SCRIPTURAL BASIS:

- **Revelation 21:3-5** — *And I heard a loud voice from the throne saying, "Now the dwelling of God is with men, and he will live with them. They will be his people, and God himself will be with them and be their God. He will wipe every tear from their eyes. There will be no more death or mourning or crying or pain, for the old order of things has passed away." He who was seated on the throne said, "I am making everything new!"*

- **Matthew 28:18-20** — *Then Jesus came to them and said, "All authority in heaven and on earth has been given to me. Therefore go and make disciples of all nations, baptizing them in the name of the Father and of the Son and of the Holy Spirit, and teaching them to obey everything I have commanded you. And surely I am with you always, to the very end of the age."*

THINKING AHEAD:

- Setting aside properties like "streets of gold" and "pearly gates," focus on the spiritual and emotional qualities and think back to what your earliest idea of heaven was.

_____

- What is the main thing that Jesus wants his disciples to do?

_____

HOW DID WE GET HERE?

A FOUR-YEAR OLD BOY finds a loaded gun under his parents' dresser. Bang! Bang! He shoots his two-year-old sibling.

In Israel, a nineteen-year-old man boards a bus knowing he won't get off. No one will. In a few minutes it blows up. The suicide bomber has lived out his destiny.

A fourteen-year-old girl goes missing from her family for more than a year, snatched against her will by cultish religious fanatics.

Four prisoners kill a guard and escape, armed and dangerous.

In Iraq, innocent children are maimed and killed by bombs set by their own people.

A CEO of a major corporation manipulates the books. He makes a fortune. Stockholders lose their retirement money.

This is the stuff of daily newscasts. We get a snack during the commercials and come back to hear the five-day weather forecast and the sports.

How did the world get to such a state that events like these are routine—and we barely feel their impact?

Our world is lost and has fallen into chaos, rebellion, and under the tyranny of the god of this world, the thief who came to kill and steal and destroy. We see the effects of that fallen, broken world every day—because it's our world. We see it on the news, we see it in our communities, in our places of work, and we've seen it in our family lives.

—from *Choosing to Learn from Life*, Chapter 3

Take a few minutes to answer these questions:

➡ What is a situation that happened recently in your own community that illustrates how malevolent the world has become?

_____

_____

_____

➡ When you hear about events like the ones described in this reading, how do you respond internally? How do you respond externally?

_____

_____

_____

➡ In what ways do you think God is present in those situations?

_____

_____

_____

AS YOU LEARN about the kingdom of God with your group, fill in the blanks in the sections below.

In the Gospels, we hear Jesus speak of the kingdom of God over and over, in his sermons, in his parables, and by his miracles. Jesus doesn't teach about a _____ kingdom that we can move to and swear allegiance to. The Greek word _____ means the kingdom or _____ of God.

It's coming and we'd better be ready! The story of the unexpected burglar in Matthew 24:42–44, the sudden arrival of the bridegroom in Matthew 25:1–13 and many other stories are pictures of the arrival of God's kingdom. It will come that quickly and change our lives that radically.

When we think of the kingdom of God, perhaps many of us think of heaven. And that certainly is a key aspect. Jesus spoke of the kingdom of God as being a future reality. Read Revelation 21:3–5.

→**HUDDLES**← *During the teaching time, Huddles extend the learning experience by encouraging interactions in small groups of 2 or 3.*

→HUDDLES← ⊙ How does the description in these verses match up with your own picture of the kingdom of God?

_____

_____

Jesus doesn't leave the kingdom of God in the future. He makes it clear that he brings the kingdom of God. Now. In this life. He casts out demons, he heals miraculously, he disarms Satan. The kingdom is here! In Jesus, the future rule of God is real. The power of the kingdom is undeniable. We know how the story will end—God will win the battle against evil—and we're drawn into the plot to experience the excitement from the inside.

If the kingdom of God is near, how do we embrace it? Jesus says two things: repent and believe.

We often think of repentance as an outside thing. "I'm going to stop speeding." "I'm going to stop overeating." Actually, those behaviors may be the result of repentance, but repentance starts on the inside. The Greek word _____ means a _____ . It describes a process of transformation that takes place inside a person.

Believe is another action word. The Greek word _____ means an active trust and taking action based on certainty you have in your heart. We show our faith in our actions.

→HUDDLES← ◐ Why is it important to put faith into action?

_____

Time. Kingdom. Repentance. Faith. These words are the heart of what it means to be a disciple. As if to underline the importance of discipleship, Jesus made a statement about discipleship as his last words before he went back to heaven. Read Matthew 28:18–20.

The word "disciple" in itself is important for us to understand. In Greek it's the word *mathetes*. The word means _____ or "pupil." Our English word "disciple" is probably more complicated than it needs to be. We tend to use it primarily in a religious setting. Actually its not a religious word at all; it's simply a word that refers to somebody who chooses to learn.

→HUDDLES← ➡ What prompts you personally to choose to learn something new in any area of your life? Do you have a different motivation in your spiritual life?

Jesus said this: Go out into all the world and make learners out of the people that you meet. If you've become a learner, then make other people learners. If you've learned how to learn from me, then go and teach other people how to learn from me. Go and disciple them, make them learners.

When we look at the Learning Circle, learn to understand these words, and apply them to our lives, we are learning what it means to be a disciple. A disciple is a learner.

→HUDDLES← ➡ How does understanding that a disciple is a learner change your ideas of discipleship?

KAIROS: LEARN AND CHANGE

WHAT ABOUT YOUR personal *kairos* event? What would it look like if the king were near? Your promotion at work, that new business deal—these present many opportunities for God's rule and influence to come into your life in a new way, affecting you family, your work colleagues, deepening your relationship with God. At that crisis point in your marriage, the king is near, bringing the wholeness that we look forward to in heaven into your daily situation. Your marriage and your family relationships could be revolutionized.

Whatever your *kairos* event, the king is near, to speak, to heal, to set free, to forgive, to restore, to influence—to rule as king! We need to learn from Jesus how to embrace it, how to get hold of it, to put our arms around everything that God wants to give us.

Jesus says we need to do two things to make the most of the opportunity: repent and believe the good news! We can only learn from our *kairos* events and experience God's rule through a process of repentance and belief. Without that process, we go from event to

event, crisis to crisis, repeating our mistakes, never seeing a lasting change. The Learning Circle describes the journey we make as we give God control of our *kairos* events and let him lead the way—the journey of repentance and belief. It is in this journey that we make our way closer and closer to the kingdom of God, becoming more like him, and drawing closer to him, with each passing challenge. It is on this journey that we can truly experience the intimacy with God and the power of his presence.

As you begin to learn about what it means to be a true disciple of Jesus you are going to be faced with a difficult challenge: use this information to simply increase your knowledge *or* use this information to live a different life. When we learn new methods of discipleship or spiritual discipline, we tend to increase our knowledge base of God and his word, but we struggle with the actual implementation and change. *LifeShapes* makes this process easier but you still have to make the choice to put forth the effort. Take this to heart as you start to dig into the deeper areas of your life when answering these questions and sharing with your group. Be ready to share in the next session about your experiences with *kairos* and the kingdom of God this week.

PERSONAL CHALLENGE

➤ What *kairos* event are you facing right now from which you want to learn?

_____

_____

➤ To understand your *kairos* moment more fully, did God reveal any areas of your life that might need changed?

_____

_____

➤ To learn from your *kairos*, what faith action do you need to take this week?

_____

_____

4 THE LEARNING CIRCLE

IN THIS SESSION, YOU WILL:

Learn how to respond to *kairos* moments

•

Explore the concept of repentance and what it means to experience change

•

Discover how to put faith into action in the context of community

•

Form a plan to apply the Circle to an individual *kairos* moment

When we're young and in school, other people usually set our goals for us and then offer us a reward for meeting those goals. This is a great way to learn how to set goals and recognize the payoffs, but later in life, we have to depend on a more internal motivation to learn and accomplish our goals. Learning is a choice. Isn't it true that it's a lot more difficult to learn something when you really don't want to, when your heart's just not in it? In the school of kingdom life, you can choose how hard you're going to work at learning from your experiences, good and bad, so that you grow to be more like Jesus every day. Learning can be tough work. You often have to pull something out of yourselves and apply it to the world around you, even if you don't really want to. The Learning Circle helps you do that.

SCRIPTURAL BASIS:

● **Jeremiah 29:11** — *"For I know the plans I have for you," declares the Lord, "plans to prosper you and not to harm you, plans to give you hope and a future."*

THINKING AHEAD:

● What is the last subject that you chose to learn something about?

_____

_____

● How do you feel when you are challenged to learn something new?

_____

its stretching but rewarding

_____

_____

KEY WORDS:

Repent
●
Observe
●
Reflect
●
Discuss
●
Believe
●
Plan
●
Account
●
Act

NO GOING BACK

YOU'RE WALKING ALONG on what you think is a straight path; no unexpected bends in the road, no intersections where you have to make a decision you're not prepared for. Just a nice pleasant stroll. Suddenly out of nowhere an unplanned situation forces you to a screeching halt. You're at an intersection now, and you have to decide what to do, which way to go. It's a *kairos* moment.

You can pretend the moment never happened and hope its consequences will go away. You can dig in your heels and refuse to move in any direction at all. You can look behind you and move back to a familiar part of the path where you know what will happen.

Or you can pass through the portal and enter the Learning Circle. When a *kairos* moment occurs, we must decide whether to enter the Circle. From the moment we step into the Circle, we are in a learning mode. Things will not go back to the way they were before the *kairos* event.

If we don't step into the Circle, we don't learn from our *kairos* events. It can be hard work to stop doing things our way and let God have total control of our lives. But when we do, we give God the space to change us and lead us in a new direction.

—from ***Choosing to Learn from Life***, Chapter 4

Take a few minutes to answer the following questions:

➡ Think about a *kairos* event in your life that revealed an area needing change. Discuss that situation and how it affected your life.

_____

_____

_____

➡ Discuss a *kairos* event in your life that you chose to disregard either by running away or simply ignoring God's prompting to change. How did that choice impact the "big picture" of that situation?

_____

_____

_____

➡ When something big happens in your life, good or bad, who or what do you immediately turn to for guidance or advice?

God, friends, someone who's gone through a similar situation

_____

_____

AS YOU LEARN ABOUT the Circle together with your group, fill in key words in the sections that follow. Label the parts of the Circle as you learn about each one. This session gives an overview of the Circle. In the next two sessions, we'll take a closer look at Repent and Believe.

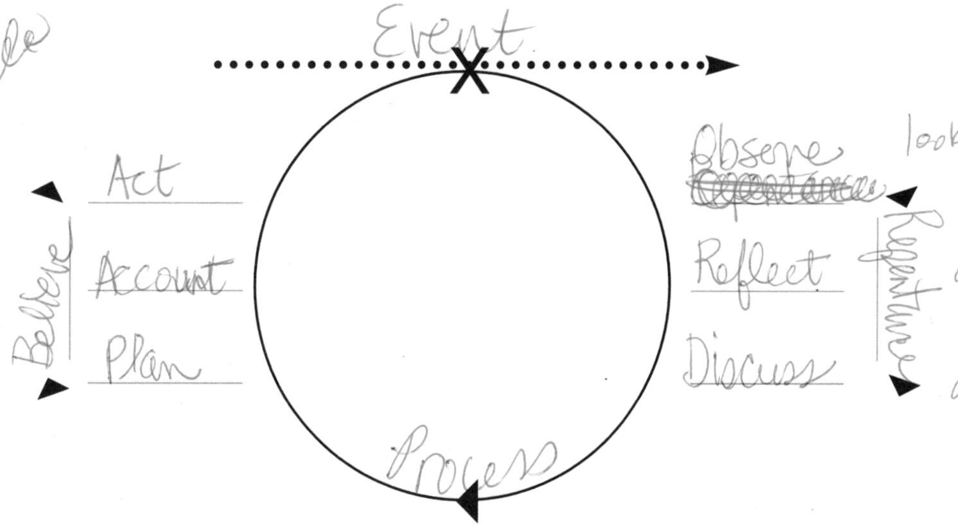

[Handwritten notes throughout diagram:]

Choosing to learn helps you become a disciple

Event

Act
Account
Plan

Believe

Observe ~~Experience~~   looks at the event

Reflect   Repentance   asks questions about it

Discuss   allowing the question to form in the air to become more concrete

Process

→HUDDLES← *During the teaching time, Huddles extend the learning experience by encouraging interaction in small groups of 2 or 3.*

We do not become disciples of Jesus and stand still. Learning means we're constantly moving and growing. Jesus tells us to do two things to make the most of a *kairos* opportunity: repent and believe. Each phase has three steps.

To start the process of repentance, we observe our reactions, emotions, and thoughts. This has to be honest observation! It's not a time to defend ourselves or blame our actions on somebody else. It is about taking a *kairos* moment and simply exploring all of the inward spiritual, emotional, or mental circumstances that led to the occurrence of that event.

→HUDDLES← ➲ How much time do you spend on a daily basis intentionally exploring your own thoughts, feelings, or impressions about significant moments?

_____

_____

After observing, we reflect. Simple questions are a good start to the process of reflection. We want to ask ourselves questions that will help us discover the who, what, when, where, why, and how of the *kairos* moment and our response to it.

Why am I feeling this way?

Why did I say that?

How did this happen?

→HUDDLES← ➡ Think of an event that triggered a strong emotional response in you. Discuss why you think you reacted the way you did.

_____

_____

After observation and reflection, it's time for discussion. Now you invite others to look at the *kairos* event with you. Other people see things that we don't see for ourselves. They challenge us where we are reluctant to challenge ourselves. The best people to discuss with are people who will be completely honest with us, even if the things they say are not what we always want to hear. Discussion is a difficult phase for people because it involves openness and honesty.

→HUDDLES← ● When you discuss *kairos* moments with someone, do you find yourself just giving the basic facts, or are you also sharing the deeper emotions and issues of your heart?

_____

_____

Be sure to add the Observe, Reflect, and Discuss labels to your Circle diagram.

BELIEVE

Learning to move successfully through the Circle means that we must learn to go through both processes of Repent and Believe. If we only do one part, true change will not occur and God is certain to allow another *kairos* moment to happen so that we can experience the lasting change he desires for us. We learn by recognizing our desire to change reflecting on that desire, but that is only the first step. Believing, or faith, means taking action. Faith, by its own definition, is active; believing in something and putting that belief into action are inseparable.

The Believe side of the Circle includes three parts:

1. _____

2. _____

3. _____

The first step in our faithful response to a *kairos* moment is to plan. Planning is about vision; it is about having an intention to do something. As you take the information gained from your observations, reflections, and discussions about a *kairos* moment, you can begin to create a plan that will affect your outward behavior. You have a vision of the end result, and you make a plan for how to get there. Making a plan is usually easy; implementing the plan is where people usually get hung up.

→HUDDLES← ➲ Taking your own personality into account, what kinds of things would help you to form and implement a plan?

_____

_____

Then, if a plan is to be effective, we need at least one person to hold us accountable to it. Lasting change doesn't happen in private. It's pretty easy to cheat on a diet if no one else knows you're supposed to be on one. It doesn't take much to spend the down payment money on a weekend away if no one knows you were saving for a home.

We all know how easy it is to point out someone else's weak points. Jesus wants us to look inwardly at our own weaknesses and to allow another person to look alongside us.

→HUDDLES← ◐ Since plans are often easy to create but difficult to implement, do you think someone holding you accountable to your plan would help you with that process?

_____

_____

Now that you have a clear plan and someone to hold you accountable to that plan, it's time to take action. Faith bubbles up within us and rises to the surface where it turns into action. Faith is always acted out, never bottled up. Take your plan off the paper and into your life.

→HUDDLES← ◐ Discuss some clear moments in your life where it was both easy and difficult to take action on a plan.

_____

_____

Be sure to add the Plan, Account, and Act labels to your Circle diagram.

In learning to apply the Learning Circle, you'll find that with your response to each *kairos,* the process of repentance and belief will lead to more of God's kingdom becoming present in your life. Each time around the Circle means that you have grown a little more and taken on a little more of the character of Christ.

SLINKY FAITH

OUR LIVES REALLY are about events connected together over time and our response to these events. The right response—repent and believe—leads us more fully into the kingdom. Once you are aware of the Circle—and put it into practice—your life will look more like a Slinky, a series of loops held together by moments in time. Every week, every day, you face *kairos* moments that challenge you to learn and change by entering the Circle. Each time around the Circle means you have grown closer to the kingdom of God, being able to experience the greater presence of Christ in your life. This is learning as a lifestyle and reflects the way Jesus lived and wants his disciples to live.

God loves you too much to leave you as you are—he will continue to break into your life with *kairos* moments in order to draw you ever

PERSONAL CHALLENGE

➲ Which part of the Circle do you think would be the hardest for you to go through? Why?

_____

_____

➲ Think about a recent *kairos* event in your life. Mentally walk through the steps around the Circle and make notes below about this experience and what you can learn from it. Make sure you end up with a plan for action.

_____

_____

➲ In what areas of your life might a *kairos* moment happen this week?

_____

closer to himself. To paraphrase Jesus in Mark 1:15, "I want you to enter into a lifestyle of repentance and faith; a lifestyle that is committed to learning from me what you need to know to be an effective representative of the kingdom. Listen to me and stay close to me, particularly in the moments I give you as opportunities to learn. Surrender to me—allow me to change you inwardly so that your attitudes and actions are constantly being renewed."

As you go through your life's journey this week, use the Circle diagram on the right side of this page to help you remember the steps you can take as you seek to grow and change in Christ. Be ready to share in the next session about your response to a *kairos* moment this week.

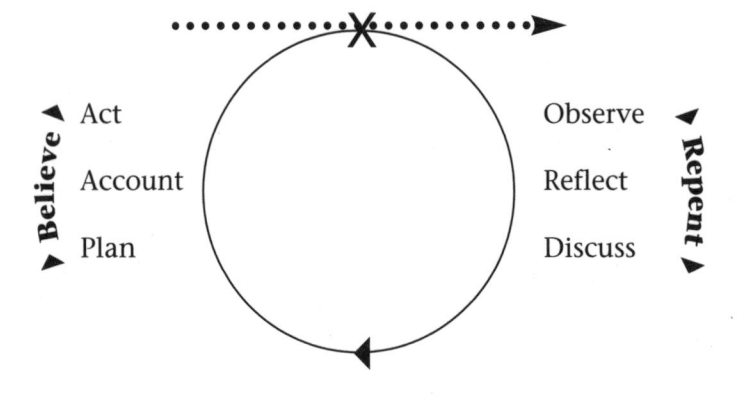

5 CHOOSING REPENTANCE

When was the last time you said, "You were right. I was wrong." True repentance is not as simple as that sounds. It's not about being sorry as much as it's about being willing to change. That's where a lot of us dig in our heels pretty deep. Change is uncertain, uncomfortable for many people. But when we open ourselves up to the change that repentance brings, we open ourselves up to a richer more abundant life in Jesus.

SCRIPTURAL BASIS:

- **Numbers 13:2, 30** — *"Send some men to explore the land of Canaan, which I am giving to the Israelites. From each ancestral tribe send one of its leaders… We should go up and take possession of the land, for we can certainly do it."*
- **1 Samuel 17:45** — *"You come against me with sword and spear and javelin, but I come against you in the name of the LORD Almighty…"*
- **Acts 9:4-5** — *He fell to the ground and heard a voiced say to him, "Saul, Saul, why do you persecute me?" "Who are you, Lord?" Saul asked.*

THINKING AHEAD:

- What is one situation where you wish you could have a "do over" opportunity?

_____

_____

- How does talking with other people help you make the changes you need to make?

_____

_____

NEHEMIAH'S DILEMMA

NEHEMIAH WAS THE cupbearer to King Artaxerxes I. This position meant that he was one of the king's most trusted advisors. One day, Hanani, a fellow Jew, visited Nehemiah and told him about the state of Jerusalem. The city was in ruins, socially, physically, and spiritually. The news about Jerusalem broke Nehemiah's heart. Even though he had never been there, this was still his homeland, the land of his heritage. Nehemiah wept, fasted, and prayed for days asking God do something.

The king knew his cupbearer well. Nehemiah was in such distress that he couldn't hide it. When the king noticed a troubled expression on Nehemiah's face and asked what was wrong, Nehemiah took a chance and told the king about Jerusalem. God's hand was at work. Not only did the king give Nehemiah permission to go to Jerusalem, but he also gave him the resources to rebuild the city walls, the temple gate, and a house for himself! Nehemiah was on his way.

Nehemiah arrived in Jerusalem and stayed for three days, watching and waiting. He went out secretly at night to look at the city more closely. He spent time observing and reflecting upon the needs of the city.

Soon it was time to share his reflections with the city officials. The officials were inspired. "That sounds good. Let's start rebuilding." And they got right to work. After just a short time, the workers grew tired. Standing in rubble up to their necks made it seem like rebuilding a wall was impossible. And they were intimidated by frequent threats of the opposition.

Nehemiah understood that if Jerusalem was ever going to be rebuilt, it would take more than encouraging words. He needed a practical plan.

—from ***Choosing to Learn from Life,***
Chapter 9

Take a few minutes to answer these questions:

⊙ We are all leaders to some extent. As a leader, what is the most effective way to present a vision to those you lead?

_____

_____

_____

⊙ How do emotions affect the repentance process?

_____

_____

_____

⊙ Based on what you know about the Circle so far, what should be Nehemiah's first step?

_____

_____

_____

As you learn about the Repent side of the Circle together with your group, fill in key words in the sections that follow.

As followers of Jesus, we are called continually to _____ how we think. Being a disciple of Jesus means constantly growing and changing inwardly. We want to be more and more like Jesus. Every day—multiple times—we have the opportunity to say, "I'm not going to be like that any more. I'm not going to snap at the sales person who can't answer my questions. I'm not going to yell at my kids about picking up their rooms. I'm not going to skip out of work early all the time." Repentance is not about judgment. It's about change.

Repentance is essential if we are to grow as _____ of Jesus, but most of the time it is not easy. Facing our failings is something we want to put off, like a trip to the dentist or bathing the cat. But hiding or ignoring our failings does not make them go away. We have to see things as they really are if we are to change inwardly.

OBSERVE

In Numbers 13 we read a story about how the Israelites got themselves into some serious trouble. Take a few minutes and scan through the chapter. Moses sent twelve spies to the Promised Land that God had promised to give the Israelites. Their mission? To observe. Look carefully and come back and tell everyone what they saw. Unfortunately, what they saw frightened off most of the people, and instead of going into the new land, they spent the next forty years wandering in the desert.

The ten spies who were frightened by what they saw in the Promised Land spread their fear to the rest of the people. Only _____ and _____ really saw what God intended them to see—the fulfillment of the promise he had made to his people.

It's easy to look at a situation and not see what is really there. Even when we start observation with the purpose of repentance and learning from the experience, we might see some scary stuff. It's not easy to be honest when we're looking closely at our own attitudes and behaviors.

When children learn to cross the road by themselves, they learn to _____ , _____ , and _____ . Sometimes we miss out on observation because we do not stop when a *kairos* event happens and really look carefully at the situation.

→HUDDLES←   *During the teacher time, Huddles extend the learning experience by encouraging interaction in small groups of 2 or 3.*

→HUDDLES← ◐ What kinds of things keep you from stopping to look closely when a *kairos* moment happens to you?

_____

_____

David was a musician, a victorious warrior, and a king who ruled for forty years. He is most remembered for something that happened when he was still a teenager. When no one else in Israel would accept the challenge that the giant Goliath taunted them with, David did (1 Sam. 17). And he wasn't even a soldier! He was just there to deliver food to his brothers. But he took stock of the situation and started asking questions. At the end of his reflections, he knew the answer to his questions: the Philistines did not have God's protection; Israel did. So taking Goliath out took only a sling and a stone.

A simple way to reflect is to ask _____ . Reflection is a common model of teaching in both the Old and New Testaments. When we ask questions about what we observe, we get below the surface to a deeper meaning of the experience.

→HUDDLES← ◐ Make a list of questions that you could ask yourself during a *kairos* experience. Make sure this list reflects your own personality and tendencies.

_____

_____

DISCUSS

In Acts 9, we find out that Saul really had a thing about the Christians. He hated them with a passion! He was on his way to Damascus, to stir up serious trouble for Christians when he had an expected discussion. Jesus himself gave Saul a life-changing *kairos* moment when he asked, _____ (Acts 9:4). Saul's answer was another question. _____ (Acts 9:5). Jesus explained the new plan. Instead of persecuting Christians, Saul would join them and become Paul, the missionary to the Gentiles. What Paul knew about following Jesus as a disciple, he learned in that conversation in the middle of the road.

We need to get into the habit of discussion. It takes humility and vulnerability with a few trusted friends. But when we do this, the path of repentance and life change becomes so much clearer.

→HUDDLES←

➡ Why do we consider honesty so risky?

_____

_____

_____

_____

NO SPACE BETWEEN US

IT SEEMS AS THOUGH our modern culture has created compartments for every aspect of our lives. We have our work compartment and our family life compartment and our church compartment and so on. We've even compartmentalized those compartments. Within our families, we've got our marriage in one compartment and our children in another. We have become a very neat and tidy society that does everything we can to keep our compartments from overlapping. After all, it would be perfectly absurd to share the personal details of our family life with our co-workers or talk to our children about a difficult time we are having at work! To make matters worse, our culture praises the principles of self-motivation and independence. The most successful people in life seem to be the ones who did it all on their own.

Yet, we can take one quick look at Jesus and realize that his life was not lived out in this way. There were no compartments in his life, there was no isolation, and there was no presumption dictating that everything he was to accomplish was going to be done entirely on his own. Jesus lived life in community. He shared every part of his life with his Father, with his disciples, and with the world around him. He always had someone to talk to, someone to eat with, someone to cry with, and someone to teach. Nowhere in Scripture is there a place to indicate a moment where Jesus wasn't doing life with somebody.

We talk so much about the need for our own personal space and privacy in personal matters, but the truth is that God designed us as people who need other people. True, there is nothing wrong with time alone to reflect or be with the Father, but the time for thinking that we "need our space" has come to an end. God created us to live in community and in that context, there is no space between us.

These ideas about compartmentalization and isolation are completely counter-cultural. They probably sound very different from the ideas of independence and self-reliance that many of us have been brought up to believe. You may or may not agree but you need not go any further than the Bible and the teachings of Jesus to see that this is contrary to the way in which our Master and Teacher lived his life. Community and transparency are at the core of *LifeShapes*. If you are going to be successful in implementing the principles of the Circle and if you are going to continue your study of the other *LifeShapes*, you will continue to face the challenges of community, transparency, and openess in your life. Be thinking in the coming weeks about this as you answer the questions and share with your peers. Be ready to share in the next session about your experiences with repentance this week.

PERSONAL CHALLENGE

➔ This is a very challenging idea. Do you agree or disagree with the ideas of de-compartmentalizing your life?

_____

_____

➔ Describe a situation in your life right now that calls for a drastic change in the way you isolate parts of your life.

_____

_____

➔ Name someone about whom you can say, "No space between us."

_____

_____

6 CHOOSING A NEW DIRECTION

"We just have to have faith." Sometimes we say that to each other when we don't know what else to do; we seem to be out of active options, so we settle for faith. It's all out of our control, so now we'll trust God. We've got it all backward! Faith is active. Faith is getting up and doing something because we have let God into our lives to change us and challenge us to commit to his kingdom work. Yes, we have to have faith. But it's not a last resort!

SCRIPTURAL BASIS:

- **Matthew 6:33–34** — *"But seek first his kingdom and his righteousness, and all these things will be given to you as well. Therefore do not worry about tomorrow, for tomorrow will worry about itself. Each day has enough trouble of its own."*

- **1 Samuel 20:14–15** — *"But show me unfailing kindness like that of the LORD, as long as I live, so that I may not be killed, and do not ever cut off your kindness from my family…"*

- **Matthew 7:24** — *"Therefore everyone who hears these words of mine and puts them into practice is like a wise man who built his house on the rock."*

even the foolish builder heard his words he just dizent put them into practice.

THINKING AHEAD:

- What's the difference between "talk the talk" and "walk the walk"?

_____

_____

- How do you feel when despite your best intentions things go wrong?

_____

_____

Jesus says "If the world squeezes you (your fruit) what kind of juice comes out? It should be Jesus juice"

NOT ACCORDING TO PLAN

YOU WANT TO BE a better spouse, so you book a meal at an exclusive restaurant. You know you need to spend more time with the children, and your mind starts planning a weekend full of together time, just hanging out, doing things your kids like to do. You know you should set a stronger Christian example at work, so okay, you're going to get right on that and start witnessing.

So you tell your spouse about the delightful dinner surprise and in return get a reminder that you have an important parent-teacher conference your spouse has told you about every day for the past week. You tell your children that you want to hang out with them all weekend, and they groan. They are all scheduled for sleepovers at their friends' houses. They asked permission, and you said yes. Now it looks like you have changed your mind. Your enthusiasm comes across as pressure to do something they don't want to do. And your work colleagues? You invite someone to church, and the person expresses a hatred for organized religion and you have no idea what to say next.

That went well, didn't it?

You were trying to live a passionate life and all you managed to do was confuse your wife, annoy your children, and alienate your work colleagues! Great!

The first stage of faith is not, "Just do it!" It is to make a plan.

—from ***Choosing to Learn from Life,***
Chapter 9

Take a few minutes to answer these questions:

➡ Give an example of how "real life" sometimes get in the way of great plans.

_____

_____

_____

➡ As the person in this story, what do you think you could have done differently?

_____

_____

_____

➡ When your plans get spoiled, are you more likely to try again or just give up? Explain.

_____

_____

_____

AS YOU LEARN ABOUT the Believe side of the Circle together with your group, fill in key words in the sections that follow.

In the last session, the final stage of Repentance was Discussion. This presents us with the chance to bring clarity and focus to the changes God wants to bring to our lives. But what happens next? You might be tempted to jump right into action. But the first stage of faith is not, "Let's just do it!" It is to make a plan.

PLAN

Remember the story of Nehemiah from the last session? The people of Israel had been in exile in Babylon for several generations. A new king allowed some of them to return to Canaan. News came to Nehemiah, the king's Hebrew cupbearer that Jerusalem was in shambles. Socially,

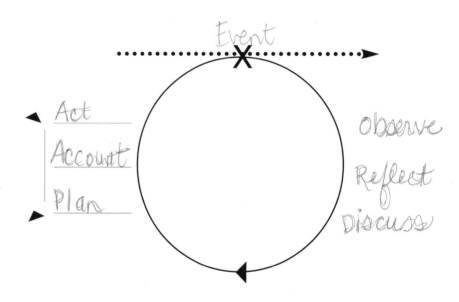

physically, and spiritually, the city was a disaster. Nehemiah was devastated and wanted to help. With the king's permission and financial backing, he went to Jerusalem to rally the people and organize the work of rebuilding the wall around Jerusalem. Nehemiah had a plan, and that's what it took to get this job done.

Nehemiah understood that if Jerusalem were ever going to be rebuilt, it would take more than encouraging words and the permission of the city officials. He needed a practical _____ that would empower the Israelite people and deal with their enemies. His plan must enable them to carry on with the practicalities of rebuilding the wall of Jerusalem as well as strengthen their identity as God's people. It wasn't an easy job, but Nehemiah stuck to the plan and got the job done.

Read Matthew 6:33–34. The key to any plan is God's _____ . We seek that first, and God takes care of the rest.

→HUDDLES← *During the teaching time, Huddles extend the learning experience by encouraging interaction in small groups of 2 or 3.*

→HUDDLES← ● In practical terms, what does it mean to seek first the kingdom of God?

_____

_____

ACCOUNT

When King Saul threatened David's life repeatedly, Jonathan, Saul's son, helped David get away to safety. But before the friends parted, Jonathan asked for one thing: "Remember that we have a covenant of friendship, and if I die, keep that covenant with my family" (1 Sam. 20:14–15).

Jonathan did die in battle, along with his father. David became king and remembered the promise he had made. Although Jonathan was dead, David was accountable for what he had said he would do. He searched for a member of Jonathan's family and found his son Mephibosheth, who had been disabled as a child. David took Mephibosheth into his own household and treated him like a member of his own family.

How many of us have started a new year with intentions to spend more time with the children, lose weight, be nice to that difficult character at work, spend more time with God, or stop speeding—only to fail by the end of the first week? If a plan is going to be effective, then we need at least one person who is going to hold us accountable for it. Remember, faith is not a private thing, and change does not happen in private.

Accountability is not someone else telling you what to do. Accountability is asking another person to help you do the things you already want to do. Your accountability partner helps you stick to the _____ you've made and take the steps you want to take. We are not forced to be _____, but we ask friends to help us by holding us accountable.

→HUDDLES←

➲ What is it about the word "accountability" that makes us uncomfortable?

_____

_____

ACT

The disciples spent three years with Jesus, learning from him and discovering what it meant to enter the kingdom of God. Eventually it would become clear whether they would act on those values of discipleship

Judas wanted to live his life by his priorities, not God's. He went to the religious leader and arranged to betray Jesus in exchange for money. After Jesus was arrested and Judas realized what he had done, he took his own life.

When Jesus went to the cross, the disciples scattered. Peter denied knowing him. Only John was present at the cross.

But after the resurrection, the disciples were ready to move forward. Before Jesus returned to his Father, he gave them a job to do, and they organized themselves to do it. On Pentecost they were filled with the Holy Spirit. For the rest of their lives, the disciples pointed people to Jesus.

At the end of the Sermon on the Mount, Jesus puts out a challenge. Read Matthew 7:24. The people who truly follow Jesus not only hear what he says but also do it. They take action.

→HUDDLES←

➡ Describe an experience when you were able to move all the way around the Circle by putting a plan into action. Have you experienced lasting change as a result of your actions?

_____

_____

DECISION TIME

YOU HAVE TO make a decision.

Action comes out of confidence. It's a faith issue.

Sometimes our lives are shaped by inactivity. We sit around thinking about what we should do, maybe even talk about how we should go about doing it. But somehow it never gets done. Underneath, we're not really sure if it's right. Or we're not sure we're up to the job, and if we procrastinate long enough, perhaps the opportunity will pass, and we won't really have to try. Or we tell ourselves we're not ready yet; we need to go back to earlier sections of the Circle. Maybe we reflect a little longer, talk a little longer, or make more plans. But there comes a point where our confidence is expressed in how we live. It is visible, it is seen, it is public. The changes are out there for everyone to see.

Jesus has always been much more than just talk. He preached and taught, but he also loved, healed, and lived among people. Every story we read about Jesus' life we see a moment where he stepped out in boldness and lived a life of action and decision. He knew that he only had a limited amount of time to impact the lives of the people he was with so he was constantly following up his teachings and observations with action. Because we're his disciples we want to live the way he lived—a life of active faith.

Be ready to share in the next session about your experiences with the Believe side of the Circle.

PERSONAL CHALLENGE

➡ What sometimes keeps you from taking that last step around the Circle and taking action?

_____

_____

➡ For you personally, in what ways would having an accountability relationship help you go from planning to action?

_____

_____

➡ Do you think it's possible to live a life of "active faith" and be successful in moving from plan to act without living in honest relationships with others?

_____

_____

➡ Think of one situation you face this week that you need to plan for and take action. How will you prepare to do that?

_____

_____

7 THE CIRCLE IN THE BIBLE

Is the whole Circle really in the Bible? All in one place? Yes! And Jesus himself uses it. In this session, you have the opportunity to stand with the disciples as Jesus gives the Sermon on the Mount in Matthew 5–7. You may be well acquainted with this passage, but now you'll look at it through a new lens. Observe how Jesus leads his disciples around the Circle—and be ready to reflect and discuss how he leads each of us.

SCRIPTURAL BASIS:

- **Matthew 6:25–27** — *"Therefore I tell you, do not worry about your life, what you will eat or drink; or about your body, what you will wear. Is not life more important than food, or the body more important than clothes? Look at the birds of the air; they do not sow or reap or store away in barns, and yet your heavenly Father feeds them. Are you not much more valuable than they? Who of you by worrying can add a single hour to his life?"*

- **Matthew 7:1, 3** — *"Do not judge, or you too will be judged… Why do you look at the speck of sawdust in your brother's eye and pay no attention to the plank in your own eye?"*

THINKING AHEAD:

- What one or two things do you worry about most?

_____

_____

- Are you better at looking at other people's mistakes or your own? Explain.

_____

_____

STARTING POINT

GO TO A CHRISTIAN bookstore and peruse the shelves that hold books about discipleship. Do you like what you see? Or are you overwhelmed by what you see? Where do you start? Bible study? Prayer? Practical theology? Small groups? Individual studies? Life topics? Book study? What's even worse is the fact that among the hundreds of books regarding the same subject matter, each one presents an entirely different idea about how to live life. Which one is the right one?

And then pick up a secular newspaper or magazine. Chances are you'll stumble across something about Christians, whether they are characterized as right wing fanatics with abortion protest signs or simply the growing bulge of middle America who claim to go to church two or more times each month.

When you decide that you want to deepen your spiritual experience, how do you even know where to begin?

The answer is simpler than you think: Look at Jesus. Learn from him. The first disciples walked the roads of Galilee and Judea with Jesus for three years. The gospels give us accounts of those experiences, so that we, too, can learn from Jesus. Every example we need to live any part of our lives as God would have us is clearly presented in the life of one man.

—from *A Passionate Life*,
Chapter 1

Take a few minutes to answer these questions:

➲ When you want a deeper spiritual experience, what kind of things do you look for to help you?

_____

_____

_____

➲ Think back to the last time that you read one of the gospels straight through in order to better understand the life of Jesus. What was that experience like for you?

_____

_____

_____

➲ In just three or four words, how would you characterize the earthly ministry of Jesus?

_____

_____

AS YOU LEARN ABOUT the Circle in the teaching of Jesus with your group, fill in key words in the sections that follow.

 *During the teaching time, Huddles extend the learning experience by encouraging interaction in small groups of 2 or 3.*

Jesus' followers have finally come to the end of another long day. Jesus has gone up on the hillside to teach, and the disciples have been listening intently. One of the disciples, Matthew, records for us what Jesus says in the Sermon on the Mount (Matt. 5—7). This is no wimpy inspirational message. Jesus is being tough. He outlines a radical lifestyle and then says that he expects his followers to live that kind of life. He doesn't shy away from the tough issues: murder, adultery, divorce, revenge, love of money, anger, lust. Jesus covers it all. If you had been there, you might have thought you were listening to a prime-time soap opera. Everyone has a secret. But Jesus knows all the secrets, and he forces them to the forefront.

So imagine you're a listener, and Jesus starts touching sensitive buttons. You start thinking about the things you're hiding. What if it all falls apart? What if you just can't hold it together a day longer? Worry and fretting set in, and Jesus knows.

Read Matthew 6:25.

→HUDDLES← ➡ **How would you respond if you were trying to hide your worry and somebody revealed it?**

_____

_____

Jesus knows what is happening in his listeners hearts, so he takes them through a process that will set them free: the Circle.

OBSERVE

Read Matthew 6:26. Jesus prods his followers to observe. "Look at the _____ ." What do we notice? We worry, but the birds don't. God feeds them, and he is going to feed us too. In observing the birds, the disciples ended up looking at themselves and their own lack of faith.

REFLECT

So they look at the birds. Then Jesus says, "Are you not much more _____ ?" Of course the answer is yes. Through reflection, Jesus helps his disciples put things in perspective.

DISCUSS

Read Matthew 6:27. Matthew doesn't give us a word-for-word record of the discussion between Jesus and the disciples. However, we do know that the usual teaching method in that day was question-and-answer. Jesus was inviting the disciples to enter the discussion process together. Read Matthew 6:28–32 for more of what Jesus challenged the disciples to think about.

→HUDDLES←   ◗ **What strikes you most about the Observe-Reflect-Discuss process recorded in this passage?**

_____

_____

_____

PLAN

So how do we build a life that is not based on worry but on faith? Read Matthew 6:33 for the clearest statement on planning that the Bible gives us. Jesus wants us to make plans for his kingdom and righteousness. Righteousness means _____ . When the rule of God comes into our lives, we let go of our worries.

ACCOUNT

Read Matthew 7:1–3. Jesus keeps us humble! He reminds us of our own frail and inadequate self-protective-ness. He's not calling us to judge each other, but to look at ourselves and remember that we are _____ for the choices and plans we make in a life of discipleship.

ACT

Let's go back to the story of the wise and foolish builders that we touched on in the last session. Jesus tells the crowd about two men. One builds a house on rock, the other on sand. Read Matthew 7:24–27. When we remember everything that came before this story in the Sermon on the Mount, starting with the Beatitudes right through to warning about false prophets, we see what Jesus is getting at. Everybody was listening that day. The ones who listen and then go out and put faith into action are the true followers of Jesus. The wise man who built his house on the rock listened to what Jesus said and then did what Jesus said to do.

→HUDDLES← ➲ **What strikes you most about the Plan-Account-Act process described in this passage?**

_____

_____

_____

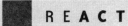
ONE STEP FURTHER

IN THE SERMON on the Mount, Jesus teaches radical ideas. He uses the pattern, "You have heard it said…but I tell you…." He reminds the people of what they already knew about how God wanted them to live. Then he takes it all one step further and demands action that will change the way they think and live their lives. If someone strikes you on one cheek, turn the other one too. If someone wants your suit, give him your overcoat as well. Don't just stay away from lustful actions—don't even let your mind think about them. Don't just pray, but pray in private so you don't draw attention to yourself. Give to the needy, but don't tell other people what you're doing.

One step further. Jesus still challenges us to go one step further. One step further in repentance. One step further in belief. One step further in discipleship. One step further into the kingdom of God.

Are your feet moving?

Be ready to share in the next session about your experiences with the Circle this week.

PERSONAL CHALLENGE

◆ Jesus asked the disciples to look at the birds of the air. What do you think he is asking you to look at right now?

_____

_____

◆ In what ways are you like the foolish builder? In what ways are you like the wise builder?

_____

_____

◆ Write about a situation you face this week that you're ready to choose to learn from.

_____

_____

8 STILL LEARNING AFTER ALL THESE YEARS

And now you've come to the crossroads! Do I take what I have learned and make it a lasting part of my life, or do I wait until something better comes along? Sounds like a powerful *kairos* moment! *LifeShapes* isn't a program that we take and practice for a few weeks before it either catches on or we decide to give up. This is an opportunity to make a permanent change in your life, and that change is simply leading you to become more like Jesus in every way. That change only comes about when you decide how you will respond to the *kairos* moments of your life. Will you respond to them by choosing to learn from life?

SCRIPTURAL BASIS:

- **James 1:2** — *Consider it pure joy, my brothers, whenever you face trials of many kinds...*

THINKING AHEAD:

- Think back over all the sessions of *Choosing to Learn from Life.* Which discussion has had the most impact on you?

_____

_____

- How has your response to life-changing events — big or small, good or bad — changed as a result of *Choosing to Learn from Life?*

_____

_____

LIFELONG LEARNERS

PEOPLE HAVE OFTEN said about *LifeShapes* that it's simple to understand, but difficult to do. Take heart, practice and failure are truly the ways that we become skilled and successful at doing anything. Do not expect to be just like Jesus after your first trip around the Circle. God gives us many opportunities, big and small, every day to work our way around the Circle. Ease yourself into it. Begin to grow and learn from the smaller moments and you will have trained yourself to prepare for the larger ones.

The Learning Circle really is the way that Jesus taught his disciples, both in the Sermon on the Mount and to all who would call themselves disciples today. In every *kairos* event you encounter, whether positive or negative, know that it is an opportunity for the kingdom of God to enter your life in a fresh way, for heaven to touch earth.

The process is one of repentance and faith. If that is the way that Jesus taught his first disciples, surely it's the way he continues to teach his disciples now, isn't it?

Take the Learning Circle into your workplace, your marriage, your friendships, your family life, your hurts and struggles, hopes and dreams. Jesus will always be the answer to your situation. The Circle is one tool to use as you dig for the presence of God in the landscape of your life. Remember, we are not achievers for Jesus, we are lifelong learners.

—from ***Choosing to Learn from Life,*** Conclusion

Take a few minutes to answer these questions:

➡ Write about a recent time when your day turned out very differently than you expected.

_____

_____

_____

➡ Identify some recent *kairos* moments: in your family, at work, in the community, at church, in a friendship, and so on.

_____

_____

_____

➡ How many times have you been around the Circle in the last day? In the last week? In the last month?

_____

_____

_____

JESUS TAUGHT HIS DISCIPLES in an intentional way. They saw the kingdom of God at work in his miracles and healings. They heard the authority with which he spoke about the kingdom of God. Jesus wanted to be sure they were connecting all the dots and coming up with a big picture of a life of discipleship. In the Sermon on the Mount, Jesus showed the disciples that the kingdom was near. Then he led them around the Circle through the process of repentance and faith.

Observation.

Reflection.

Discussion.

Planning.

Accountability.

Action.

This was the way Jesus taught the first disciples. Surely it's the way he continues to teach his disciples. We are his disciples, we are his *learners*. He has called us to a life of learning from him and then teaching others what we have learned. If we fail to learn (which includes change and growth) from him, we will fail in our call to make disciples out of others. The Learning Circle can be your tool; not just a tool for learning about the process of change, but a tool you can use to implement true change in your life.

Just as Jesus wanted his first disciples to learn their way around the Circle, he wants you to learn your way around the Circle as well.

During the teaching time, Huddles extend the learning experience by encouraging interaction in small groups of 2 or 3.

→HUDDLES← ❷ Which one of the six parts of the Circle has had the most impact on you? Explain.

_____

_____

The more times we go around the Circle, the more familiar we become with the process. We recognize *kairos* events more quickly. We move more smoothly into the repentance process. Experience teaches us that while planning and accountability can be a little scary, we can succeed and have a positive result. While once we applied the Circle to the larger issues in our lives, now we see that we can apply it to the smaller things that happen to us, perhaps even on a daily basis.

→HUDDLES← ❷ Has the Circle become easier for you as you've come to understand it more? Explain.

_____

_____

The Circle becomes a tool that we carry with us every day, everywhere we go, in every relationship, in every circumstance. It's the right tool, and we want to keep it within reach at all times. When we pull it out and use it, we see more and more of the kingdom of God—the rule of God in our lives, right now and right here. At first, some of the steps of the Circle may be very difficult for you to work through. As you make a conscious effort to practice these steps and to share your knowledge with others, you will find that the Circle will start to become an integrated part of your life.

➔HUDDLES←

➲ How has studying the Learning Circle changed the way you look at ordinary events?

_____

_____

_____

➔HUDDLES←

➲ Has there been an extraordinary *kairos* event in your life to which you can go back and process through the Circle? This process may reveal some change in your life that God wanted but that you overlooked.

_____

_____

_____

THE EXTRAORDINARY ORDINARY

REMEMBER THE SLINKY? We said that discipleship is like a Slinky. Life is a series of loops connected together by time as we go around and around the Circle.

One of the most fun things to do with a Slinky is to set it up so it will "walk" down a set of stairs. It's a mesmerizing experience. How does it do that? Sure, if we stop to analyze the physics of it, we could give a technical explanation of force and motion. But it's still cool to see! We set it up again and again to see if it will "walk" again.

You may feel at times as if you're going around and around the Circle and not moving forward. Perhaps you think you've learned that lesson enough times. Why doesn't God move on to something else? Or would it really be so bad just to walk a straight road for just a little while?

When you feel like that, remember the Slinky. It does move forward. The pace is not always steady. We watch while it seems to lean over the step precariously—and then it goes! Just when we think it's going to stop, it goes one more step. Discipleship is that way. It keeps going, even when we feel like the pace is slow. God is at work within us. His kingdom rules within us. He takes ordinary events and makes extraordinary learning occasions out of them. When you're inside the Circle, you can be sure you are moving forward!

<u>PERSONAL CHALLENGE</u>

➡ Name one lesson that God has taught you that was difficult for you to learn. What finally made the difference?

_____

_____

_____

➡ How do you feel about how fast your discipleship Slinky is moving at this point in your life? Explain.

_____

_____

_____

➡ Make a plan for how you will apply the Learning Circle in your life in a consistent way.

_____

_____

_____

CONCLUSION: CHOOSING TO LEARN FROM LIFE WORKBOOK

You've just had your first glimpse into one aspect of Jesus' life that sets a precedent for how we should also live. Indeed, the Circle is simple to learn but difficult to follow—we often ignore opportunities in life to change because we just don't want to face the challenges involved. Be encouraged; start with those smaller *kairos* events and get used to the steps you have to take to get through them. As the Circle becomes more and more a part of your daily routine, you will discover that it begins to come naturally in all those significant moments.

As you have studied the *LifeShapes* Circle, many of your examples have probably been focused on certain behaviors or attitudes that you want to change in your life. Changing the way we behave in our relationships, careers, or home life is usually only the first step. God wants to get into the deeper and hidden parts of our lives, he wants us to explore the true depths of who we are and why we are. The Circle has now equipped you with an excellent tool to help you in every part of your life. Don't be afraid to use it. God is looking for disciples who are authentic and transparent. The depths of applications for the Circle are unending. You will use this tool for the rest of your life and still not experience all that it can show you. But that is the true nature of your life as a disciple of Christ. Be a lifelong learner of all he has to show you!

You may wish to continue your *LifeShapes* adventure with an in-depth study of the Semi-Circle. *Living in Rhythm with Life* will cut to the very heart of what our culture has taught us regarding the relationship between our work and our rest. Check out **www.LifeShapes.com** for more information and release dates. You will come away from this book feeling challenged to take that next step toward living a passionate life for Jesus.

The Word at Work
Around the World

What would you do if you wanted to share God's love with children on the streets of your city? That's the dilemma David C. Cook faced in 1870's Chicago. His answer was to create literature that would capture children's hearts.

Out of those humble beginnings grew a worldwide ministry that has used literature to proclaim God's love and disciple generation after generation. Cook Communications Ministries is committed to personal discipleship—to helping people of all ages learn God's Word, embrace his salvation, walk in his ways, and minister in his name.

Faith Kidz, RiverOak, Honor, Life Journey, Victor, NextGen . . . every time you purchase a book produced by Cook Communications Ministries, you not only meet a vital personal need in your life or in the life of someone you love, but you're also a part of ministering to José in Colombia, Humberto in Chile, Gousa in India, or Lidiane in Brazil. You help make it possible for a pastor in China, a child in Peru, or a mother in West Africa to enjoy a life-changing book. And because you helped, children and adults around the world are learning God's Word and walking in his ways.

Thank you for your partnership in helping to disciple the world. May God bless you with the power of his Word in your life.

For more information about our international ministries,
visit www.ccmi.org.

A Passionate Life
Small Group Resource Kit by Mike Breen & Walt Kallestad

This Nine-Lessons *LifeShapes* ™ course will help small groups break new discipleship ground. Through the DVD teachings, stimulating group and interpersonal discussion, and homework applications, groups are encouraged to stop doing discipleship, and to start living as authentic disciples of Jesus. Groups will learn how the basic shapes (Circle, Semi-Circle, Triangle, Square, etc.) of *LifeShapes* will help them recall and follow Jesus'example in every spiritual and personal aspect of their lives.

A Passionate Life Small Group Resource Kit
ISBN: 0-78144-279-6 • Item # 104443
1–Paperback edition of *A Passionate Life*
1–Leader's Guide
6–Workbooks
1–DVD-9 Teaching sessions with *LifeShapes*™ creator, Mike Breen

Additional Books, Leader's Guides and Workbooks available

To get your copies, visit your favorite bookstore, call 1-800-323-7543, or visit www.cookministries.com.